An antho...

PAINT US

RED

Women of the World

Special acknowledgments to Sean Whitty Photography for the
cover art's anatomical reference and inspiration, as well as Pixabay
for several interior illustrations in this publication.

Caught Red Handed

caught red handed, a phrase first used
in reference to people caught with
blood on their hands from murder.
used in modern english to apprehend
someone in the course of wrongdoing.

to all the women, wrongfully
marked, apprehended, blamed, accused,
judged - let you be unafraid
to become all that you are.

let us, as women, take back our worth,
our belonging, our power.
let us name this movement: reclamation

PAINT US RED.

Contents

Caught Red Handed

when i was sixteen,
i knew all the things
a young girl should not know.
i knew hate for my body.
i knew resentment for my mind.
i knew bitterness towards my life.
i knew suffering.
we're oftentimes afraid
to put explicit labels to such ailments,
but today i will be brave,
and be the voice i wish i heard
when i was younger.

i knew body dysmorphia.
i knew anxiety.
i knew depression.

today i know these things still,
but i do not welcome them.
they are no longer wanted
as guests in my home.

- Cassandra Wood
[@cm.writer]

11

as women
we are taught,
from our very first breath
to never use our lungs,
to never be loud
or make ourselves seen.
we are taught
that our voices
do not matter,
our opinions
do not matter,
our wants and needs
are unimportant,
we do not have the power.
but i am my mother's daughter,
and from childhood's hour
i was taught to speak.

- Helena Degn
[@helenadegnpoetry]

do not shrink yourself
to fit into the space
between 'pretty' and 'nice'-
when they tell you that
you taste like syrup
and sound like springtime,
show them just how
hard you bite.
do not doubt that
you are made up
of elements that can
both drown them
and let them breathe;
you are the moon
and they cannot stop you
from moving seas.

- Sian RJ Wilmot
[@srwpoetry]

i did not cry wolf
(not this time)
and now i wish
these rivers of doubt
would drown me in the dusk
set me free
from the shame
that follows me
from another man's misdeed…

he thought *i* was the one
who needed to meet love
as if those promises (of forever)
were mine to keep.

as you slipped between the sheets
to greet me
i was somewhere in-between;
    a sheep led astray
unaware everything
was about
to change.

i'll never smell 3 am rain the same,
walking home

to collapse into the frame
of another bed
crying wolf to the pillow
fading like a fragile ending.

one day at a time
(i still feel the silk -
finding the hidden
road he took
before i could speak)

how i reminisce (of innocence)
looking back under cold water
" w o l f "
        i should've screamed.

i am not a girl anymore
        barely human.
                i did not cry wolf.

instead i become one;
a dangerous woman
untamed
and ready to reclaim
what i lost
to the night.

                - Cassandra Wood
                [@cm.writer]

lightning strikes my flesh
and i shudder as electricity
disperses through my bones.
the threat of annihilation
is whispered against my throat
by the thunderstorm above me.
the clouds are falling again,
careening towards the earth,
and i'm afraid i won't be able
to seek shelter fast enough.
i'm growing tired of holding
shattered pieces of myself
in my bare hands.
i'd rather destroy myself
than let this whirring storm above
destroy me first.
even as i plead for mercy,
the thunderstorm wraps
it's ice-hold hands around my throat
and squeezes until the air scampers
from my lungs.
i'm growing weary of watching
even the mirror shy away
from my reflection.
i've felt peace nestle into my collarbone,
trying to shove kindness into my mouth.
and i swallow every time
because maybe one day
it'll make a difference.
maybe one day i'll be able to tame the thunderstorm
and teach it to love instead of loathe.

just like i was taught
to love instead of loathe myself too.
just like i was taught
to swallow lies instead of truths
and pretend they tasted the same.
i'm turning blue from the cold.
the ice is settling in,
the thunder rages above,
and i can't breathe without frost
coating my lips.
annihilation has returned again,
pulling the flesh from my bones
and drawing the blood from my veins.
i resemble a corpse
with a beating heart.
i have no strength to fend off
the thunderstorm.
but strength has never come
from my blood or my bones.
strength has come from my heart.
and while my heart still beats
behind my ribcage,
making peace with the thunderstorm
is not entirely impossible.
making peace with myself,
however,
may prove to be
the most difficult task
of all.

- Adelle Woods
[@adelle.woods]

one night i dreamt of a pale hand driving a dagger
through my stomach like a heartbroken juliet

and when i woke up i was
b l e e d i n g

not like that though. more like extra strength advil
and angry red blossoming through white seventh
grade jeans - angry tears at how the school nurse
started calling me a woman when i felt like a girl.
angry that i had just discovered a less pretty world
where womanhood meant that i had to be careful.
children do not like to be careful. girls do not like to
be careful. women should not *have* to be careful
about a million different things nobody else has to
worry about.

- Arumann Dhillon
[@akdpoetry]

i dip my fingers
into the garden of
eden. it feels so
good, i don't know
how it can be wrong.

self-pleasure is not only normal, but healthy.

- Alexandra Espinoza
[@alexandramichellepoetry]

another full turn of a year
in this heat, i feel
                    and feel
                            and feel
the pangs of guilt,
so let's free them from the cage:
dearly sorry
for once rejecting this afro,
this tree from my father,
for hiding from the sunlight tan lines
and the impatient, wishful scrubs
at my skin - which was different,
the small town girl who wanted to fit in.
i hug you.
in time you will learn.
dearly sorry
for hearing the taunts so young
and swallowing its sour taste.
asked for sex appeal so early,
asked to be modest for respectability,
asking my bones to become comfortable,
covering and hiding from the unwarranted.
dearly sorry
for the pressure of youth
for finding only mud and misguidance.
left for you to solely clean,
as your own mentor, saviour
goddess.

dearly sorry
that through all this
poetry came to sing,
but the crows now fly away
and here come the songbirds
so you can write their melodies
in your memories
for the next fifty years.

- Gigi Wickham
[@isorosawords]

men always want to hear what i have to say,
paving my way to the podium
silently anticipating the words to spill
from my lips, like sweet honey onto
their laps, until
they learn that it is not them i want, no.
that is when they begin to strip me
of my dignity and peace
when i become the bitch in their stories
the whore they curse under their breath
ripping the voice from my throat
revoking my right to ever speak
that is when my sanity comes to question
when my truth is twisted into lies
because their needs are god-given rights
in which they're entitled to
at the expense of anyone who dares to disagree.
men always want to hear what i have to say
until they don't.

- Elizabeth Todoroska
[@tipsyloveletters]

22

when did my choice,
become your judgement?
i'd really like to know,
because my voice is beginning to waiver,
and my heart is beginning to hurt.
please, show me mercy, and answer:

when did my choice, become *your* judgement?

- Cassandra Wood
[@cm.writer]

jealously and competition
programmed into our blood,
unaware that society uses it against us
to keep us in the box into which we are born.
but if we came together
to fight the true cause of our downfall
we could take back our position
as the true heroes of the story.

- E.J Sneed
[@ejsneed]

half
of me thanks papa for his teachings,
you must be harder to overcome such sensitivities,
the world is not pleasant you see.
don't cry now, you are not unique
as this is not unusual,
don't be a martyr to being human.
i look to my brother, does he even feel a thing?
calm and collected he stays.
i learned the art this way.
half
of me reminisces
on the times i was scolded for tears
or even the simple word 'no',
meaningless as the paperweight on the table,
only holding weight when it serves the user
who doesn't want their things out of place.
my discomfort unimportant
then explained away
by mensuration or lack of logic.
it grows harder to stay open
to believe instinct when it lays
right on the pillow, denying sleep
in favour of believing this is all
dramatic theatre.
then harder to cry, rather burying in books
and drink and ignorance.
where is the love?
where is the middle ground?

                    - Gigi Wickham
                    [@isorosawords]

can't you hear my silence crying?
why don't you listen?
don't just watch.
should i be flying high in dreams or demise?
or at least trying to do something gratifying
instead of sighing and vying for some quiet?
it's intensifying, like the sky before a storm...
listen to me lie.
listen to me ask, "why?"
listen to everything i do not say.
because one day, i will no longer pray
to a god i do not believe in,
to a stranger who's in danger...
and that stranger is me.
it seems to be i am to blame,
for this shame and my tamed spirit,
my tainted name... i've lost this game of strife.
the life of perfection is a sharp knife.
i am trapped,
because i only attract chaos and madness,
because i am flawed,
because i am only a facade,
because i want to change
but instead,
only stay the same.
can't you hear my silence dying?

- Cassandra Wood
[@cm.writer]

my imperfections make me real.
my mistakes teach me to grow.
my dreams give me hope.
my faith makes them come true.

- Shefali Dang
[@theshefalidang]

he says he's a poet, with such antics so frantic
he recites words he's rehearsed to make you think
he's well versed in being romantic.
recycled remarks salivating to swim the atlantic
dripping onto your screen
to make your heart trip gigantic
with intricate phrases
stealing so many sighs,
it's been identified many times
as slightly asthmatic
letting those rows of landlocked lungs
wave white flags to his tongue, surrendering none.
lust must be deadly fun, and for some
sin is bound if it sounds cinematic
just don't let yourself be held down when he
dances around and out of this manic
love's beat, cannot breathe in these basements
please, bring it up to the attic
and put some light on this sight
you will find you are fighting with static
his true colours have crawled onto your canvas,
proven polychromatic
the cat's out of the bag
his idiopathy, you see, is idiomatic
with disguised idolatry drowning
in the baths of babble, so automatic
because the bullshit he spread
from the pit of his bed

is getting aired, getting said
it's so aromatic

frequently fleeing from flirting with speech
founded in the flames of a "screeching fanatic"
as he takes a swing with the scar
of another girl's heart
being labeled dramatic
i guess when he promised me honesty, it was just
symptomatic
of side-hobby sweet talk
unlocking serenaded charades, so sadly systematic
but we are on to his ways, that premeditated praise
his sheets will burn in our blaze
tossing and turning under his lies, every cover
discovered
as we rise…
beyond the untruths that are treading traumatic
he says he's a poet
he's problematic.

- Molly Gentzsch
[@themusingsofmollymaven]

they clip my wings,
and tie me up;
they seal my lips,
and smother my soul;
they rule my thoughts,
and judge my grace by the size of my clothes;
they blindfold my eyes,
and feed me lies;
they fetter my feet with chains of shame,
and entitle me weak and fragile;
they make me fall to my knees,
and ask me how it feels to be free;
but with a choked throat,
how do i tell them?
that amidst the mayhem of their terms and taunts,
i have forgotten the taste of freedom.

    - Maryam Asad
    [@miserable_writes]

we wear it in our hips
by the way they sway
with each step we take.

on our chest when it
softly bounces with
any sudden quake.

between our legs when
they spread (to be pleased)
causing them to shake.

in our demeanour when
we carry shame, after
every single mistake.

with our actions, trying
to please everyone else
with choices we make.

we wear it like a skin,
because as a woman
you never get a break.

being a woman is the new scarlet letter.

- Alexandra Espinoza
[@alexandramichellepoetry]

i learned to look down
when they look at me.
i learned to pull my shirt up
my sleeves down
my skirt below my knees
because if any ounce of my flesh
is revealing itself
it no longer belongs to me.
i learned to stay silent
when they are around
never speak too loudly,
have too many opinions,
share too much information,
because no one wants
to hear it from me.
i learned to do as i'm told.
don't ask too many questions
i don't need answers
if i just follow directions
i'll be fine,
right?
but each day i grow older
i learn to unlearn
all these stories and myths
these horrible lies
poured down my throat.
my body is my body
look away if you're hungry

i'm not a meal for your eyes to eat.
i am loud, and i'll get louder
with each day that passes
i'll scream until your ears bleed
and you'll listen to me.
i will never stop wondering
stop learning
stop asking
stop following my own
path i create.
i am a woman
i am a woman
I AM A WOMAN.
and i belong to me.

- Kaileigh Pfaff
[@kayf.j]

if you have to judge me
judge me when my soul is at peace
and mind at rest
not when chaos has me handcuffed
and put itself in the driver's seat
when my eyes are smiling
and twinkling in joy
not when they are sunken in defeat
and the light is barely there
if you have to judge me
judge me when i've made it through the darkness
and i'm basking in the sunlight
not when i'm sinking in quicksand
unable to see the right from wrong
if you have to judge me
judge my whole book,
because a page does not define me

- Shefali Dang
[@theshefalidang]

there is nothing more powerful
than a woman who cannot be defined-
who says you can't be both
sunshine and cyanide?

- Sian RJ Wilmot
[@srwpoetry]

Never Enough

i find myself at a tug of war
with the girl in the mirror,
fingertips bleed through
as calloused palms grip
an invisible rope
fighting over
who i should be
and
who i am.

- Elizabeth Todoroska
[@tipsyloveletters]

i stood in the mirror,
hating every inch in the reflection,
repeating the words, i've heard before.
every critique, every unsolicited opinion
about the body i live in,
trying to make myself the woman
only i wanted me to be.

- E.J Sneed
[@ejsneed]

i tried to write about that night. about what happened and how i felt when it happened, hoping the words would spill from my hands and i wouldn't have to feel it anymore. but instead, i lay in this bed, felt my muscles get tense and my hands shake as i listened to the sound of my quivering lips gasping for air. i can always feel my lungs crushing under the weight of all these thoughts on tuesday mornings. i don't like tuesdays. my eyes well up as i stare at the ceiling, but i don't cry. sometimes it hurts too much to cry. you don't like watching me cry anyways. i know you don't, because every time i do, you just turn your face and pretend you don't see me. instead, i make my way to the shower, the cold water rushing over my back is numbing to more than just my skin. it helps distract me. and my left foot is bigger than my right, have you noticed? i guess it's fitting, nothing about me ever seems to fit together. symmetry is a sign of beauty and i just want to feel pretty so i scrub until my body turns red hoping it'll change something - anything. maybe if i wrote about you in something other than a love letter i'll learn how to love me enough to leave. but some things aren't so easy to express and sometimes i'm not ready to write about things i want to write about. so i'll save your poem as a draft and write it another day.

- Elizabeth Todoroska

[@tipsyloveletters]

keep your chest up.
stay youthful but
appear grown up.

suck it all in.
be virtuous even
while you sin.

stick your hip out.
just smile more
and somehow pout.

pose just right.
try to be modest
yet not so uptight.

appear perfect.
we want natural
without defect.

societal contradictions.

- Alexandra Espinoza
[@alexandramichellepoetry]

we are born into a box.
boxes within boxes,
each with their own label
telling us who to be,
until we believe
that we are unworthy,
of love,
of living at all...
until the only box
we feel we will fit in,
is the one in the ground,
six feet deep under soil
when we can't breathe,
because the cracks between the wood
aren't enough.
haven't we endured?
haven't we succumbed?
we try our best to fit,
but we never will.

- Cassandra Wood
[@cm.writer]

43

my favourite colour
would be pink
i would spend my days
at the kitchen sink

manners and dresses
would be all i know
i'm expected to always
come through for you

maths and science
will take time for me to learn
thus cooking and cleaning
are the tasks i've earned

i wouldn't dare
to ever show scorn
all this, is what you decided
on the day i was born

this poem is simple
i wrote it for you
to make it easy to understand
that i'll only do what i want to

i'm a being of my own
i won't let my fate be decided
to the men that walk past me:
i have now presided.

- assumptions

- Janhavi Purkar
[@janwritesx]

bottles / they hold what we need / inside / staring at
that liquid courage / those numbing doses / my
thoughts and their long / goodbyes / glass, plastic,
skin / break them, shake them / give my soul the
whole of what / begs within / and i will always
remember / the farewells of december / rooms of
black cloth / crowding the remains of faded
embers / i have walked these coaled roads / before /
all the pebbles thrown at stones / and bones / under
my feet they lay in soiled / doors / adorning bullet
wounds, necktie / tombs, those breathless bound
bodies / i will join them soon missing suns / of
june / to wear the dirt that / dances / on mahogany /
oh, death / how you have kissed my lips / we fell in
love / a tryst that grips / i have shed many tears,
given / many years / but my better moments will
just / scratch at walls / tongues split, mouths will
spit / only one second of my life to be / recalled /
and as i swallow my no tomorrow / the world turns
despite such / sorrow / so, let them say / all i was /
became this day / but i will count the petals /
plucked, the nights so tight / warm and tucked / the
red blanket that burned him / into me / the embrace
that laced / his charring charms to my / heart's race /
how we cried at the finish line/ miles of smiles that
were never /mine / they belonged to a girl / i once
knew /but these dusty mirrors will not get / much

clearer / i'm now made of glass, it shatters blue / a bottle emptied, a covering coffin or dust confetti / i am nothing more / and everything / with the smell of smoke on my last breath / i choke to sing / the letters of words which / welcome death / a parting note that spoke / of all the reasons why, i had fasted / hope / a taste these jaws would gladly / soak / yet, they hang bare / unable to greet the stale air / please, know that i am home / as the sky pulls me to fly / i've woven my wings, a refined magpie / no longer bottled by / the tegument that ties / some rest for the restless / this is why / the dreamless die.

- Molly Gentzsch
[@themusingsofmollymaven]

i've written my monologue
in the Book of Sacrifices;
every remaining blank page
meant for the next handover
to the next woman
hoping to be the last.

- our story

- Janhavi Purkar
[@janwritesx]

how cruel.
broken girls
know everything
they should not.
she gives her all,
tries her best,
but is left
nothing
but broken,
again
and again.

- Lena Mora
[@iamlenamora]

"she looks so happy"

the woman in the painting
sits with her head high
she is dressed
in a blush pink with
seams of gold glittering

her arms are heavy
as if she is holding
the weight of all her
unsaid confessions

she wears sadness in her eyes
it is a secret the brush
strokes can not disguise;
expression crossed between
silence and love

strokes of love
are smudged in the
crease of her eyes
and yet somehow
every time you gaze

into her eyes
all you see is grief

bits of hopelessness
collect in the corners
of her ghosted smile

the harsh discordant
mixture of colours
haunt her expression
see me
hear me
feel me
the colours bleed

the slump of her shoulders
pushes into her body
heaving with the unspoken truth
expressed by each stroke
and yet it remains
concealed to the world

of all the lies ever
witnessed by my eyes
hers were the loveliest
                    - Aaisha Hanif
                 [@poetrybyaisha]

51

my mind is at war with my body.
    but who started this war?

too many nights wishing upon superstars
like shooting stars
with an empty plate
    slowly drowning in silence as i wait
as i wonder
"how many calories have i ate?"

i'm sad i'm broken again,
    lies slipping through my teeth
like silk.
    "i'm fine," i say
as guilt crawls beneath my skin.
i feel like somebody else.
falling
        in
            reverse
with a double knotted tongue
and a fake smile,
too late (again) to take it back:
what i said to my body that day,
who was just trying to stay alive
as i resented it for not fitting right
in those blue jeans
from the eighth grade.

i want to disappear (but please notice)
as i critique
    my every move
        every meal
            every mark
                every little thing that makes me
                  real.
i never loved my first home
because
i was never shown how to love it;
only hate.

i was taught every remedy for
    red skin
    bloating
    stretch marks
    (none of which require fixing of any kind at all)
and not the medicine i truly needed:

self love.

but that's not profitable to the media
so i've got none.
i've gone numb.

- Cassandra Wood
[@cm.writer]

the gaze, a thing only turned off by a blink or sleep
but there are eyes where eyes cannot see
inside skull
inside hipbones
down to feet, leaching into blood
from the soil of this land
that is dictated by desire.
the loss of meaning of what is beauty
turning her into a slave.
that phantom weight creeps,
a centred scale to check its validity
an illusion it is, but the counting down is real.
to breaking.
of the eyes
of the ears
of where the grass is greener,
and by the time you are lulled into this dream,
it catches you and keeps you for its tricks.

- Gigi Wickham
[@isorosawords]

we're used like doormats
and expected to smile,
while they get all the credit
for the floors being clean.
        - uncredited

            - E.J Sneed
            [@ejsneed]

she peeks - into the mirror -
at her body
at the curves that wrote her destiny
with tired eyes she watches
vacantly at the flesh
that no longer feels like home.
with a heart of melancholy
she feels change
wash over her like a storm,
changes the eyes cannot see.

she wonders who she is (anymore)
with a crying heart seeking to break free.
she wonders
    how it would be
        if she hadn't gone out that night,
(looking like the highest majesty)

because when men like him see women like her
an angel in hell
he comes running
to destroy (everything).
oh - how painful a story of angels can be.

that night somebody touched her secret paradise,
turned it into a frozen tree

she's crying
holding on to the mirror
where her secrets become truth before her eyes
only for her eyes...
she died inside (but still lives for the world)

the morning of that day
she woke up to find strength again
with a hopeless, heavy mind.
she was given the title
victim
from the rape of the last night.

the little angel
doesn't feel the same anymore
they crushed her halo
they destroyed her garden.
her body mourns
her heart refuses to love
this world
the one that makes life a hell
for a warm woman like her
they turned her heart cold.

- Lena Mora
[@iamlenamora]

i blanket hope
over this bruised soul
my smouldering heart; broken
with the love slowly pouring from the cracks
it showers acceptance
upon these seasoned scars

- Marie Claire
[@s.m.claire]

dear you,
do not lose your true colours,
to suit their cooler tones.
never try to grow
in places flowers are not welcome.

- Maryam Asad
[@miserable_writes]

on the edge of a cliff
i reminisce about flying freely through the clouds
departing from the heaviness of the world
preparing myself to take the plunge
into the depths of the vast ocean
i look to the sky;
with one glance from the stars
they light a path back home
the very place i know
my soul will always shimmer brightly.

- Marie Claire
[@s.m.claire]

the stretch marks on our thighs
telling a story of growth
so soft and tender
yet we feel less sexy revealing them
the hair on our legs
telling a story of rawness
so wild and free
yet we shave it all off
the fat on our hips
telling a story of richness
so curvy and feminine
yet we try to get rid of it

how could they ever tell us
these things are not beautiful?
while these are the very things that make us so
magnificently and unapologetically human

- Lindy van Hillo
[@lindy.v.h]

we are taught
to be silent
to be submissive
to be pretty and always thin.

we are trained
to be feminine
to be a mother
to be a wife and to please men.

we are expected
to be demure
to be sensual
to be abstinent and never sin.

but there is so much more
to being a woman than this,
harness your confidence within.

to all my young girls.

- Alexandra Espinoza
[@alexandramichellepoetry]

she tells me that skinny
tastes better than chocolate,
but my skinny tastes like
a glass of water for breakfast:
cool stream pooling at the bottom
of an otherwise empty well.
like trying to run the mile in five minutes,
copper pennies underneath my tongue,
gummy vitamins quenching midnight
hunger: too much of a good thing
can be deadly.

~ and i prefer the chocolate anyways

- Arumann Dhillon
[@akdpoetry]

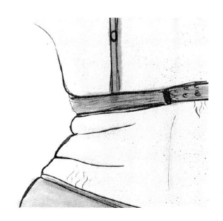

If God was a Woman

you cannot handle the chaos of women
we are fire starters; the creator of man
when you worship God, you worship our wombs
yet you have the audacity to deem us lesser than.

take yourself off the damn pedestal
and put us on it instead
show us the kind of respect
you show your mama

we brought your fragile masculinity into this world

and you best believe
we can take you out of it too

> - Helena Degn
> [@helenadegnpoetry]

tell me a rape joke
and i'll give you
a reason to gape, joke.
i'll shave your head
in your sleep, joke.
i'll show you my teeth, joke.
put flies in your tea, joke.
tell your mom
you're a creep, joke.

and the next time
you open your mouth
to make a rape joke
you'll choke
on the words and
remember that women
don't find your hands
around their neck

particularly funny.

- Arumann Dhillon
[@akdpoetry]

if given a daughter
i will gift her a clever tongue,
sharp in the face for all those that reach to tear,
a resilient ego
and a poised resolve
to gracefully move forward.

- Gigi Wickham
[@isorosawords]

perfection is ugly.
where is the beauty in holding on tighter and tighter
to the blade of a sharp knife, the very tool you use
to cut the most beautiful parts of yourself away?

there is no admiration, in cookie cutter existence.
there is no joy,
no emotion,
no passion.

authenticity is your most beautiful form.
seize that instead.
use the knife to cut the rope around your neck.

breathe again.

- Cassandra Wood
[@cm.writer]

mountains will crumble at my feet
when they see the woman
i have become.
stars will shift out of alignment
when they hear all that
i have done.
the rain will fall for me
and flowers will mistake
me for the sun.
oh, when the moon howls for me,
how the wolves
will run.

- Sian RJ Wilmot
[@srwpoetry]

she placed her crown
on her dragon wings
and set fire to the sky
there is no lie in her truth
she is both woman and wild.

- Aaisha Hanif
[@poetrybyaisha]

i am a
daughter of the earth
of mother nature
my soil is my soul
when my soil is
watered with love
and nurtured
i burst into flowers
from dust just like her
i wilt and wither
under harshness like her
i grow like her
i evolve like her
i shiver in the frigid cold
i love unconditionally
i even look like her
for i am the colour of earth
and one day i will be
one with her

- Shefali Dang
[@theshefalidang]

womanhood will not be her demise,
it will be her uprise

thunder holds her hands
lightning paints her blood
the fading glittering in her eyes
is a clear raindrop
falling on a cloudy spring day
they say more to earth
than her lips ever could
all that hurt she holds in her chest
a pain so bound and writhing in her heart
can only be collected in empty exhales

watch as kingdoms and kings
fall to make room for her reign
there is bravery in her blood
she painted her white flag
in blood and raged against the world

- Aaisha Hanif
[@poetrybyaisha]

i find the footprint i made when i was two,
young and new,
eating honeydew, exploring meadow rue…
… that little girl, she didn't know,
how she would grow,
the places she'd go,
about the sunshine and scraped elbows.
she placed her toes so firmly into that paint,
living without restraint,
because she wasn't yet afraid
of what the world would tell her…
society was not yet her saint.
sometimes i wish i could go back,
to the brave faced,
painted-feet girl,
and capture her excitement;
her innocence.

- Cassandra Wood
[@cm.writer]

say what you will
let those tongues sharpen
let blood be spilled
i am not meant for silence
i am not meant for lying under
lidded daffodils
i have embraced the shadows
i have caressed his thorns
hollow horns have had their fill
to be ravaged, the sentimental
savage, the damage
too much pain to be bested by
my benumbing pills
black wings once encumbered me
how the dark, (hide her spark)
could impart a start to my heart
for it no longer feels the confinement
of bestill
i have awoken, not your token,
not broken

i have unburied my voice
it has spoken
and the red that has spread from
my mouth to my head
has given breath to the dead
the swallow, the swill
so, gather your swords, play me
your chords
ignite the ignored
and see your eyes bleed
at the cuspate of my quill.

- Molly Gentzsch
[@themusingsofmollymaven]

they'd look at her
in confidence
whenever she had
a decision to make

only because they knew
that with her timidity
she would easily break

to learn that
freedom of choice
does not remove one's
fear of failure

meant she had to choose
between herself
and those that called themselves
her saviours

- *undecided*

            - Janhavi Purkar
              [@janwritesx]

i am more than
black heels and a short dress
red lips and hair pushed back
more than a rumour you heard
in a crowded bathroom or over brunch
more than a story or experience or
a statistic you can conveniently hurl
to push your political agenda
i am life and love,
the mountains, the sea
and everything in between
i hold the world in my palms
and the heavens dance across my skin;
you do not get to define me

- Elizabeth Todoroska
[@tipsyloveletters]

too many days i have prioritized my modesty
over my personal comfort.

- Cassandra Wood
[@cm.writer]

hands are meant to hold
not for you to intrude on my skin
breasts were made for nurturing
not for you to stare at and grin
lips are meant for tenderness and love
not for you to catcall on the streets
legs were made for walking
not for you to forcefully grab between the sheets

your body is not meant to control mine

- Lindy van Hillo
[@lindy.v.h]

i was born
in the midst of darkness,
the place where
nightmares
reign over the restless.
i was born
with a noose around my neck,
but i will not allow
my life to end in that way.

don't blink
or you'll miss just how ruthless
i can be.
i am a girl, a woman,
with blades lining my sleeves.
blood has never
tasted sweeter
when it falls
like rain.

i'm fairly certain
i could be your worst
nightmare if i really tried.
crawl into my skin,
my home,
and you'll see the extent
of the wreckage here.
i haven't forgotten
the way blood has trailed
from lips by your hand,

by their hands,
by even my own.

depending on which way
the light reflects,
you'll either glimpse
the victim

or
the villain in my eyes.
a nightmare for you
and all who stand
before me.
a promise of pain
to those who dare
try to and cut me down.

yes,
i am a nightmare
with a daydream on my lips
and i won't hesitate
to bring this war
to your doorstep.

'I KEEP A RECORD OF THE WRECKAGE IN MY LIFE'
(inspired by Halsey's song nightmare)

- Adelle Woods
[@adelle.woods]

sometimes empty
sometimes whole
half mind
half soul
a little scattered
a little sorted
sometimes peaceful
sometimes chaotic
black and white
with rainbow shades
this is me
this is my world

- Shefali Dang
[@theshefalidang]

girls like
her
you
me

were born with a birthright
to seek and experience eternal happiness
to choose freedom and explore our femininity
to never be judged and condemned
for the definition and directions of womanhood.

- Aaisha Hanif
[@poetrybyaisha]

ghost girl
lost in the woods of her mind
with a language
nobody can find
alone but not lonely
escaping from time
and the demons that chase her.
but this forest is alive;
the earth tree is calling
with a voice only she can hear.

"in this journey of life
there is great pain
and you must heal,
from the karma
you must connect
to the life you live - seize it!
don't hurt anymore babygirl
because something is seeking
the forest of your mind,
the language of your heart.
slowly this soul of yours
will find the truth of this universe"

ghost girl
found herself in the woods
alone but never lonely.
                    - Lena Mora
                    [@iamlenamora]

she's a princess
in a tall tower
with dragons that heed to her
and respect her power

she yields a sword
to protect herself
and those that need her,
she'll fight for them as well

her warriors are women
like her mother who raised her
able to look into a man's eyes unafraid
she's proud of them now and who they once were

together, we'll change
her voice stronger than ever before
our tower will keep growing,
like those that we fight for

- in her crown

- Janhavi Purkar
[@janwritesx]

[daily affirmations]
1. my inner goddess is powerful and magical.
2. i love living in my beautiful female body.
3. i embrace being a woman because if i don't - who will?

- Mansi Jora
[@tiara.less]

over the years,
i have learnt
that i must never fear my voice.
though it quakes
and i ache
for my shortcomings,
i now know that
this skin,
this body,
this heart of mine
will always
be
my
home.

- Adelle Woods
[@adelle.woods]

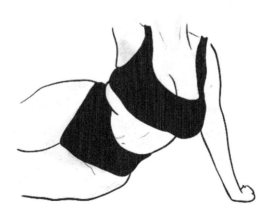

on fresh cut grass i walk barefoot
grounding myself
and connecting my mind to the lessons
the earth brings
to the vastness and nutrition of soil
as i feel the green stroking and tickling
in between my toes

in the ocean waves i swim
freeing myself and letting my heart trust
the flow of the water
to surrender to the ebb and flow
that comes with life
as i let the different shades of blue
carry my body peacefully

in the wind i breathe
to let my soul sigh alongside me
as i feel the breeze playing with my hair
imagining the air brushing
through my being
to let the wind communicate
with all that needs a fresh breath in me

in the sun i sit silently
letting the warmth contact my skin
as i let it spark my passion
i don't have to move
for the fire is spreading
to the corners of my fingertips
making me feel alive inside

i am earth water fire and wind
all existing within me
as a tiny little part of our nature
and as i let myself become one
with my surroundings
i know i am just another fragment
of this intrinsic beauty
so i let all the elements fill my soul
allowing myself to be whole

- Lindy van Hillo
[@lindy.v.h]

i will pick the door handles
to the room that carries my heart
and decorate the walls of my mind
with memories of every soul's parts
i will exhibit the places i've visited
through my eyes like souvenirs on a shelf
so they all become a reminder
of where i found home in myself
for every time i see new faces and places
i leave pieces of my heart behind
so the parts i give to someone else
will be replaced with what i find
and sometimes it will be heavy to carry
because i am no longer made up of me
but of all the other things
that my windows have made me see
sometimes they let me see the sun
and yellow strokes paint my insides
other times they let me see the moon
so black and white control my tides
some hearts used all their black paint
and covered me with more dark than light
their brushes stroking my walls
now carrying the stories others write
i collect words and tears and laughter lines
like paint strokes swallowing me whole
it will be the most intriguing art piece
forever hanging as a canvas in my soul

- Lindy van Hillo
[@lindy.v.h]

NOTE TO SELF

fall in love with yourself first,
and the world will follow.

- Cassandra Wood
[@cm.writer]

if these walls could speak
they'd tell me

don't. be. weak.
pick yourself up and fly
quickly dear
 there's strength
  in your soul
   rise from the floor
soar and see
 all of the world
  we will never
   get the chance
    to meet.
do it for me.
 (the room echoes and i begin to breathe again)

- Cassandra Wood
[@cm.writer]

we are the stars in the sky
the ocean waves crashing on shores
and the lava spilling from volcanos
we are all the earthquakes
and the thunderstorms
there are legends written about us
tales of mythical creatures
with blood between their legs
who have birthed the most powerful of men
behind every great man is no one
before him is a goddess
and she will not be overshadowed.

- Helena Degn
[@helenadegnpoetry]

am i not enough?

not enough
to feel the sun, the shadows or the light
that shines so bright.
just because you judge me day and night
for who i am…

am i not enough?
as a woman who gives birth
to angels for this world?
i raise heaven as a roof for us.
how am i not enough?
with my tears i water the fruits you possess.
and i - a woman - in the comfort of the night
become your dreams and the night's light.

how am i still not enough?
stranger worlds call me a goddess alone.
an ocean offers to be my home, sky as my blanket
with the stars above.
they pray to the sun to keep me loved.

but you still think i am not enough!
i help you find paradise
when you are completely alone
when nobody is there - for you.
but me (your shelter).
i'm growing tired. i'm done.

mother, how am i not enough?
i've waited for this moment to speak loud

instead of letting silence drown,
those voices that yell from my chest
every morning are trying to break out.
yet i am still here mastering loneliness
and wondering why am i not enough?

i call you for the last time
and this time i yell
    i am not just flesh
    i am more than what you say
    and what you can imagine

you tried to pick the most beautiful flower
from the garden of my soul
without compassion
without gratitude
without respect.

but today i yell: *i am enough*
because i am not a simple flower
i am me, a woman, who helps the moon shine full.
i am enough.
the moment i say it, my lost power returns.
today i am strong
i give all my love to me
because i will never ask my soul again
why i am not enough for you.

this time i am enough for me
        - Lena Mora
        [@iamlenamora]

could it be
they were threatened
by the strength
of the woman
or maybe
they were jealous
that she was closer
to god than any man
could ever be
because it is her
who is caressed
by the hands
of the universe
it is her
who receives
the gift
of a second heartbeat
could it be
that they realized
the power
of the woman
and had to find a way
to take that power back.
        - and yet, we continue to rise.

            - Kaileigh Pfaff
              [@kayf.j]

i'll fight 'til i conquer my fears.
mute my sound,
hold me down,
but i'll scream 'til my voice is found.

- Maryam Asad
[@miserable_writes]

i've never chased a happy
ending
or any ending at all
i'm the needle that needs
mending
but despite all this bending
i don't hear hands at curtain
call
every stage i walk upon
i pretend the lights will never
fall
but in that minute that i saw
you
i started breaking down the wall
as a child i hunted spotlights
those starry-eyed midnights
that tried to keep me small
until i learned that we're all
actors
reciting lines that our minds
want our hearts to recall
these mistakes we remake
aspirate
lungs lined with our flaws
i'm coughing up the restless
i'm fracturing my jaw

because your clapping feels
endless
your palms are red and raw
for once i'm happy to be
helpless
the way you make me love me
has left an audience in awe
so kiss my mouth to breathless
your air is the only drop of
heaven i'll withdraw
what we create is deathless
when we touch
cannonball.

- Molly Gentzsch
[@themusingsofmollymaven]

my body is encased with tinted glass.
the world can't see in but i can see out.
this is the only way i survive.
i am a fire hazard;
the world is gasoline.

i burn hotter than the sun
when summer rolls around.
the february heat
may be hot enough
to ignite the ground
i walk on,
but i am a fire hazard,
so proceed with caution.

death sits on my shoulders
like a bird perched on a ledge.
if the temperature is high enough,
the glass surrounding me will burn
and leave me with nothing.
the same way
this world
has left me with empty palms
and a cold, lifeless heart.
i am a fire hazard
but even the ice
within my flesh
refuses to melt;
the force of coldness
is unmatched.

find me in a cage where the sun meets the sea.
the only thing that can stop me from blazing a path
all the way to the edge of the world
are the ocean waves before me.
i am a fire hazard
with fuses for hands.

humans are vengeful beings.
we twist our darkness
into something tangible
and wield weapons
we're not meant to.
i've burnt myself one too many times on my own
flames not to be a danger to every person i meet.
i am a fire hazard
and the world falls
at my feet.

not only does the tinted glass
protect me from them,
but it also protects them
from me.
they can't see just how dangerous
i really am.
and i can always see
when they get too close.
i am a fire hazard
and i have everything
to lose.

                        - Adelle Woods
                    [@adelle.woods]

you need no permission
to depart from the life you are living
and start again.

- Cassandra Wood
[@cm.writer]

the barriers they built around us
are begging to be broken,
but it's in your hands
to destroy them.
          - shatter the glass ceiling

                    - E.J Sneed
                     [@ejsneed]

i don't need him to love me,
but i've decided to carry my heart in my empty
hands, to fall apart, to depart and start (again), to
chart new territory and be brave as i pass it to him,

(the chambers of my soul, blood filled with lunar
power as i cower at the midnight hour)

i wish only to hide my face from you (i place it
against your chest). it is as if this falling (in love), is
a constant collapse. because to this day, i feel
selfish, afraid (of the vulnerability that is love), of
caring so much that i   might   just   fall   apart
or tumble from this tightrope.

but I AM NOT WEAK.
this love may wash over me like a riptide
and wash me to new shores of change,
this newfound softness in my soul
is not weak (or small) or frail or fragile
it does not make me "less than" to love fiercely.

but beneath this all, i am afraid of sacrifice...
of losing what i have only just found:
        the feeling of a home in my own soul
         in my own mind
         in my own body.

106

and now the house is on fire.
you shout from the basement, the wooden
floorboards howling as they splinter, begging for the
safe retreat of living unloved… of living in a reality
where what dreams become are what they already
are: dreams (fleeting)

when the fire dies, i will never know, it was you
who started the blaze, because i am too much of a
woman for you to praise.

i need not pray for the day i will rise,
in the ashes of who i once was,
departing from the embers of your
burnt corpse (that haunts my mind)

ghosts cannot love (properly)…
and at the end of the day, that's all you ever were:
the ghost of a man i thought you could be.
   of the man you'll never be
because you were only a man
who took and took and took (from me).

ghosts cannot love properly,
but a phoenix can
and as i fly (reborn once again)
i cry an elegant song:

i don't need him, to love me.

                              - Cassandra Wood
                                [@cm.writer]

what is a life spent wondering
if the grass is greener on the other side?
go see for yourself.

- Cassandra Wood
[@cm.writer]

to my body:
i forgot to thank you
for allowing me
to plant a seed in you.
i forgot to thank you
for the scars
on my belly
that remind me
that even though
you didn't have it
you made the space
for my seed to grow.
i forgot to thank you
for keeping
my heart beating
through the
excruciating pain.
i forgot to thank you
for making me a mother.
and giving me
my most cherished
gift of all.

 - an overdue love letter.

- Kaileigh Pfaff
[@kayf.j]

georgina off highway 48,
there are tall sunflowers, a farm of the brightest
surroundings.
thinking my blood too sullen for earth's gifts,
its beauty would sweep over my eyes
as quickly as storms that carry lightning
that strikes just as you blink;
the light retreating behind pillowy clouds, so you
miss the bright
when drenched in undertones.
i think of such shades of femininity.
my mother tried pink on me, she tried the flair of
dresses,
on a child whining,
to a teen denying,
as an adult emerging, was it ingrained all along?
i did not think it cliché.
i did not think of girlish glee as weakness.
i thought weak was in this space i stood
flashing in and out of the laws of girlhood.
an angst filled court
and as a courtier, i play the games
the tests are always narrowly passed.
they glazed my sight
with white and grey
(i can stand in both shades).
i've always been filled with some longing,
how can these coexist?

the sweet tones of a giddy girl,
light, bright,
perhaps as far as manic pixie.
and then there's the sombre
grey, brown, blue
and the shadow of all shadows, midnight black.
i retreated to unpack all i've carried:
a girl must smile, be pretty and please,
be sweet— i stopped dead at that object
but what is sweet with no bitterness?
we wouldn't know the difference.
femininity is light and joviality
but how can that be without their opposites?
i appreciate colours more now, they suit me
i will try and pick these sunflowers softly
because now i know i'm not coded error
for these cycles of gloom
that turn to most intense peaks.
i have felt the shade before
picked a rose and kept its thorns
i can have them both,
and i smile at that little girl
who sipped on melancholy and hugged corners.
i say to her now "see the sun and the storm, the coal
and the gold".

- Gigi Wickham
[@isorosawords]

i will lay among blankets of sun,
and quilts of daisy patches,
to remind myself that i too…
am growing.

- Molly Gentzsch
[@themusingsofmollymaven]

one day,
i was contemplating the world,
and i vowed,
that i was not beyond repair.
i dug my feet into the soil,
reached deeper with my toes,
and let them become roots.
grounding myself, the earth delivered,
the affirmations i needed for my wounded thoughts,
to mend.
i discovered the courage and clarity i needed,
to heal, and bloom.

- Cassandra Wood
[@cm.writer]

We Rise Together

and just like that
the darkness collapsed
to let the light through.
all it took was for me to
finally look at myself
and say
i love you.

- Shefali Dang
[@theshefalidang]

i have spent far too many years ripping myself
at the seams in order to try and create
something you would find pretty,
as if pretty was something needed to be achieved,
as if pretty wasn't something i already was

i would bleed from my knees, dipping my
fingers in the crimson red paint, smearing it
across my lips and across my cheeks,
grinding my bones on rocks
to be a size you find appealing

but life is not meant to be lived this way
and i am tired of living my life for you
of twisting and turning my body for you,
and so,

i am beginning to learn how to stitch myself back
together
needle and thread weave through split skin as i
lean down and kiss it better, i will love you,
i will.

- Elizabeth Todoroska
[@tipsyloveletters]

she finds depth
in her imperfections
she is in love
with her truth;
in the rarest sense
she is one
with every missing piece
of her heart
where the light
shines easier and washes
every shore within.
she embodies this luminosity
with her hair of gold
and a mind of flowers
she is otherworldly;
the master
of the bridge
between heaven and hell.

- Lena Mora
[@iamlenamora]

119

why the obsession with flowers?
it is simple, really.

they are thought of as fragile and beautiful.

much like a woman.

yet, no matter the condition, they flourish and
thrive.

much like a woman.

and when harsher seasons arrive to knock them
down,
they return in the spring more glorious and vibrant
than ever.

much like a woman.

- Alexandra Espinoza
[@alexandramichellepoetry]

dear me,

when you curse at the impurities of your mind, i will trace my fingertips along your scars and remind you that they are the drawings of your soul. when you let the water fall from your eyelids, i will show you the rivers that flow through your veins and remind you that rivers overflow after heavy rain. when boys masquerading as men have entered your heart, i will have my chisel ready to create crevices in the stone so the layers of concrete you thought you had to build will crumble. in every moment of darkness, i will be here to remind you of the passion that makes flames dance across your skin and to show you the light in your soul that bubbles like champagne on a hot summer evening. i will be here to let the sweet juice of your heart flow out and let it run down the cold glaciers that have formed themselves inside your ribcage. i will always be tucked away in every corner of your being to remind you that you, my darling, are a *force*.

- Lindy van Hillo
[@lindy.v.h]

the beauty of roses
are their thorns.
darling, your flaws
make you.

- Lena Mora
[@iamlenamora]

let your teardrops water your deepest wounds
and watch them sprout,
watch them bloom.

- Cassandra Wood
[@cm.writer]

fall in love with authenticity
bask in the sunlight of new beginnings
let the petals of your soul reach for the sky
fall in love with living
for the truth of each day
and let your flowers bloom.

- Cassandra Wood
[@cm.writer]

some days, i yearn for my mouth to be able to form the words that would tell the world of what he did; there'd be wildfires in the shape of women in the streets. i know that i would have arms to comfort me. i would be listened to and believed. but it's been months and the words are still stuck in my throat. i spend nights choking on them, trying to spit them out to an empty room. perhaps speaking of trauma is like learning a new language for the first time, perhaps before i try to form sentences, i must learn how to count to ten. perhaps articulating what he did is a spark that must be kindled until it is an inferno, until it is roaring and raging and ready to go. the only phrase i can speak in french is 'my name is' and the only sentence my trauma speaks is 'i was my own home until he tore me to the ground'. maybe one day, i'll wake up with the vocabulary to explain how it feels to be hurting from the inside out. maybe i won't. i have come to peace with the fact that, either way, that boy will burn. i have come to peace with the fact that, either way, i will rise from the ashes of the destruction he made. i will never be the same. but i will be okay. i've made it through another day.

- Sian RJ Wilmot
[@srwpoetry]

125

when i was younger i could scream
so loud, crowds of crows would

s c a t t e r

from the twisted aspen trees in every
vancouver playground. i walked alone,
then on crackling branches, arms stretched
on either side of me, bare toes gripping the sap
soaked bark, wind rolling underneath my wings
it carried my laughter in it's little dance.

is it possible
to be more alive than little girls
who carry pieces of the sun and
everyone in their smiles?

- Arumann Dhillon
[@akdpoetry]

i never knew grace
i will go down screaming
guns blazing, uncaring
i am not a good little girl
i will tear down the ceiling
and stand with the ones
who do not know the same
privilege and freedom as i do
our voices are too loud
screaming 'me too' and 'time's up'
i never knew grace
and i will not be complacent

- Helena Degn
[@helenadegnpoetry]

breaking boundaries
we're told to lower ourselves
so they will always have the advantage
but it's time to show them
how high we can climb.

- E.J Sneed
[@ejsneed]

guard your heart if you must
but never bolt it shut
for loneliness will
destroy all promise of happiness

      - Marie Claire
       [@s.m.claire]

a perfect mixture of rainbow and storm
she is tangled like chaos and serene like calm

- Maryam Asad
[@miserable_writes]

do not be ashamed,
your body is exactly how it is supposed to be,
cherish each curve, each line, each fold,
you are a goddess,
be bold.
be vibrant and be kind.
do not be ashamed,
only proud of the person,
you are continually becoming,
let the things that rest out of your control,
simply float away and transform from worry,
to pride.

- Cassandra Wood
[@cm.writer]

131

you spit *witch* like it's
a dirty word
and that is why
you will never
be overcome with the
feeling that you are
made from magic;
that is why your flames
will only ever warm me;
that is why you
will never be able
to comprehend
how i can rise
and rise
and rise again.

- Sian RJ Wilmot
[@srwpoetry]

she speaks with the sky and dances with the stars,
she finds peace in her chaos
and comfort in her scars.

- Maryam Asad
[@miserable_writes]

i notice his phone ping
and watch him smile as he reads the text
we're watching a movie
and i swear i don't mean to
but when he goes to the bathroom
i look through his messages
and i see your name
and for a moment i'm furious
and i hate you
how could you try to take
what is mine and not yours

but when he comes back
it occurs to me that you
are not the villain here
this boy is
he is breaking my heart
and leading you on

so when i can
i get ahold of your number
and shoot you a text of my own
"hi, you don't know me," it says
"but i'm about to dump (name redacted)
he's not worth my time
and he sure as hell isn't worth yours either"

three years on and we call him
the traveling douche
and we are the sisterhood of his sorry ass

- Helena Degn
[@helenadegnpoetry]
134

you gave me promises
and dreams
both false and broken
another one of your schemes

you gave me dresses
and jewels
only the ones you approved
like a doll made to follow your rules

you gave me kindness
and generosity
so sudden and unanticipated
it was only when you wanted from me

i gave you everything i had
with no one else to give to
you took it all for granted
it's her job to make do

when i could finally see
the orange suit
i broke apart the bars
and left en route

you should've known better
than to treat me as a sitting duck
now you're an empty puppeteer
oh how i'd love to see you dumbstruck

- metal bars

                    - Janhavi Purkar
                    [@janwritesx]

you see, that's where you're wrong
my desire to be more than what they expect of me
to be more than just someone's somebody
never has and never will be
my detriment

but you,
your need to prove your superiority
will only leave you
broken and bruised
with your heart sore
wishing your life meant something more

- Elizabeth Todoroska
[@tipsyloveletters]

[she is for her]
this is my fight against the patriarchy -
it would be powerless,
if i did not demand it (equality).

many she(s) and many her(s)
come together to support
many of us.

the change we seek resides within the women,
for how we behave towards ourselves
is to each other.

- Mansi Jora
[@tiara.less]

standards inscribed,
by whose authority? not known.
becoming a limited collective judgement.
have you ever seen
how brown eyes are honeyed by the sun?
with skin to match, smooth as the fountain of youth,
their fountain marble white;
sable or ebony will not do
but why?
if its water allures
as curls do when they capture the wind
releasing a springy bounce.
have you ever seen full soft lips
that sing softly when cooking?
the very lips imitated at every turn,
they hum on mockingly
at how they have grown to be loved.
oh and the intellect, the courage
passed on and on,
determined to overcome
and they haven't rid us of us.
the pride bell is still rung
recalling the mothers who instil black girls with
confidence,
and the skin sisters who then go on
to uplift one another.

in a world where we are cast aside as bizarre
and unappealing, we chuckle.
it is enough of a reason
to flaunt the unique.
we are like a fifth season, and
in some future time they will see it.
and if not
then we will scream it
(for ourselves)

       - Gigi Wickham
       [@isorosawords]

yes, we are angry. angry that we live in a society
where a girl's youth is plucked at the ripe age of
thirteen. where children are seen as women from the
moment they reach puberty. trading in their
skipping ropes for newfound sexuality. angry that
advocating for our safety is seen as a radical push
for female superiority. angry that they have chosen
to point their fingers at the clothes she chose to wear
and not her perpetrator. as if it was the soft fabric
that drew him to her. a piece of cotton twisting
around his neck. manipulating. persuading.
seducing. losing all control. no. he chose this. and
the truth is it doesn't matter how many oversized
sweaters she wears, it doesn't stop their lingering
touches and stares. we've been hearing it since we
were fifteen, "oh, honey. you'd look so much
prettier on your knees." so yes, we are angry,
because everyone watches him slip his hand onto
her inner thigh, she's sixteen (but it shouldn't
matter) no one says anything. but they see. they
always see. they just don't care, do you?

- Elizabeth Todoroska
[@tipsyloveletters]

you filled my lungs with air
when breath escaped them
those full moon eyes glistened a path
through my heaviest storm clouds
reminding me that mountains
are made to be conquered
although our timing
a villain we could not defeat.
on my own
i now stand tall
upon this moonlit peak
with only your whispered guidance
dancing through my veins

- Marie Claire
[@s.m.claire]

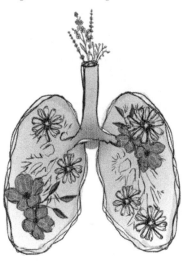

never allow
the love
you have for a man to
let him believe
he owns your body.

- Lena Mora
[@iamlenamora]

empty eyes are waiting,
waiting to be filled with joy,
from a reflection.

how silly.

do not search for happiness in a mirror,
in a measure,
in an image surreal,
an idol to which you kneel,
without first realizing,
it is not about what you choose to reveal.

why don't you fill them
with something real?
heal.

take a moment and fill those empty eyes,
with the world.

- Cassandra Wood
[@cm.writer]

they plotted us against each other;
an unnecessary proxy war
they wanted us distracted
they wanted us detached
for if we were unified,
they'd know we'd win for sure.

- the battle we chose not to fight

- Janhavi Purkar
[@janwritesx]

she was born with it.
a wild spirit,
a fierce soul,
a heart full of adventures,
a dream,
and a hope.

she was born with it all.
a power in her thoughts,
a magic in her bones,
a passion in her blood,
and a voice to own.

she was born with a light and a spark,
she was born with flaws and scars.
she was born with a fire and a desire,
and she was born to embrace it all.

- Maryam Asad
[@miserable_writes]

when i was a little girl,
i was told stories,
of princesses,
locked in towers,
cowering as the dragon outside,
ceased to sleep,
waiting for the day her prince,
would arrive,
to save her.

but i vow,
for all the little girls,
who thought,
"i am more!"
more than a girl in a tower,
who awaits the day,
of her saviour's arrival.
i vow to rewrite the stories,
the ones we tell our daughters
unaware of the potential,
melting from their souls
to their feet.

i vow to write the stories,
and shout them loud,
of the girls who ride dragons
for fun,
and who fly into the sun
for their own glory.

imagine how powerful,
that generation will be.

- Cassandra Wood
[@cm.writer]

some try to sail towards their horizon
as quickly as possible
until they find that their horizon
isn't something they can ever reach
some stop in the harbour for a while
and seek home elsewhere
until they are ready to set sail
and continue the journey
some let their anchor sink into the sand
to float in the same waters
until they are strong enough to carry the anchor
inside of them

everyone copes with pain differently
but we all have the same ability
to heal

- Lindy van Hillo
[@lindy.v.h]

i'm not sorry that this is controversial,
i will give no apology for believing,
that fundamentally,
a woman should have the choice,
to rule her own life,
to prioritize her life,
to make this intimate choice,
without the noses of white men,
lurking within her uterus,
deciding for her,
a choice they'll never understand.

- Cassandra Wood
[@cm.writer]

we have been told
our whole lives to sacrifice.
sacrifice for our family.
sacrifice for our husbands.
sacrifice for our children.
sacrifice.
our happiness.
our hopes.
our health.
sacrifice.
but who will sacrifice for us?
when our hands are bleeding.
and our feet are swollen.
when our hearts are heavy
who will carry them for us?
sacrifice.

when we grab for what we want
we're slapped on the hand, shame on us.
for wanting. for wandering. for wishing.
but what does that teach those
who watch us?
who learn from us?
to put yourself last?
to stunt your own growth?
that needing and wanting as a woman
isn't the same as needing and wanting as a human?
are we not human?
sacrifice.
truth is, the sacrifice of women's
skills, voices, strength, guidance, knowledge, love
is a sacrifice we're no longer willing to make.

   - Kaileigh Pfaff
    [@kayf.j]

she is powerful.
she is powerful enough to drown you
with a pinky finger in the sea of
love and care.

she is resilient.
she is resilient enough to lift you
with a pinky finger from the trench of
pain and depression.
      - i am she

      - Mansi Jora
      [@tiara.less]

starting over
a blank canvas
inspiration flows
from wild flowers and the velvet sky
my brush strokes creating a masterpiece
that has always existed;
concealed inside my homeless heart

- Marie Claire
[@s.m.claire]

i choose to rise once more
and let myself roar.
you tried to silence my thoughts
my voice even more
and i let you.
now i need to hear myself
loud and clear
because my voice
wasn't meant to be
just inside my head.

- Shefali Dang
[@theshefalidang]

i will never be all bright and gentle
why do i pretend to be?

to be good and conventional,
when i am a girl with a
heart covered in butterflies
free as the boundless sky
and an untamed soul
rooted deep into the earth

i'm growing into all the
colours of uprooting.

- Aaisha Hanif
[@poetrybyaisha]

It's a Wo(man)'s World

---

look at her now
wounds transformed
into words and wishes.
she realized
that not all queens
wear crowns;
she rose from the ground
and found
a love within her soul.
it crashes passionately,
peacefully.

- Cassandra Wood
[@cm.writer]

dreamers live differently
with a bit of magic in their eyes
with a little more madness than sanity.
a woman like her (a dreamer)
makes hell taste like paradise.

- Lena Mora
[@iamlenamora]

there is a fire
a deep sense of longing
inside of me
the voice of my soul
urging me
challenging me
to discover newness
and bring freshness into my life
to become only what i can;
the best version of me.

- Shefali Dang
[@theshefalidang]

i have neatly folded your name
and buried it inside the raggedy box
sitting atop my dusty bookshelf
a small box that holds once loved memories
with your name now tangled within the contents
i navigate this journey without you
blooming from my tears
and echoing breath into my lungs
i will shine brighter on my own!

- Marie Claire
[@s.m.claire]

the sun lingers in the sky / as night time falls / chaos descends into the air / wildflowers halt their blooming / i falter / lose sight of the ground / i no longer feel safe here / confined to my own skin.

wake me when i am at peace / when the sky no longer falls at my feet / wake me when the sun streams daylight / not darkness / and this coldness disperses from my bones.

this land beneath my feet / my palms / my restless body / trembles / in fear / we are all afraid of something, but fear feeds the wildflowers in bloom / as long as the moon / continues to love the sun / unconditionally.

i bloom under the sun / shed layers of my skin until i am anew / fear flees at my command / and safety returns to its rightful place in my hands / i am fighting for a better world / and a place to always call home.

- Adelle Woods
[@adelle.woods]

all that twinkles isn't light.
sometimes it's a fiery enthusiasm,
waiting to outshine the stars.
sometimes it's a free bird,
waiting to meet the horizon.
sometimes it's 'she'
seeking the warmth of love,
not to satisfy her desires,
but to fuel her passion.

she seeks the strength of compassion,
not to be confined by protective layers,
but to hold a hand as she soars.
she seeks the liberty of trust,
not to be stuck with a label,
but to set her free.
she seeks a love that will not suffocate her breath,
a love that will not cage her hopes and dreams,
a love that will not build walls around her heart,
a love that will not mould her into something
delicate,
for she doesn't like to be owned by anyone but
herself,
she wants to be loved not possessed.

- Maryam Asad
[@miserable_writes]

you collapsed into a burst of stardust
and mended into something beautiful
claim your pain
rise from the fire
you were created for chaos
you are beyond man's comprehension

- Aaisha Hanif
[@poetrybyaisha]

i asked helen of troy
if i was worth her namesake
she said:
"you survived a war you started
and didn't need anyone's help
no one is more worthy
than you, my child"

- Helena Degn
[@helenadegnpoetry]

walk to the store.
whistle, whistle.
ignore.

go on a short run.
honk, honk.
ignore.

dance in the bar.
smack, grab.
ignore.

tan by the pool.
gawk, gawk.
ignore.

post online.
dm, dm.
ignore.

simply just exist.
catcall, catcall.
ignore.

stop harassing us.

- Alexandra Espinoza
[@alexandramichellepoetry]

i do not give my love lightly
for my heart dances with the avalanches
such snow that briskly blinds in its burying,
ever brightly
cracking the ribs,
his cradled alabaster on crimson cribs
holding beats of faith,
so slightly
and i would be remiss,
as not to blanket with my kiss
the untrampled tops of
marvels, a mouth carved from mountain's tips
lips i have sought and conquered, nightly
and what is in a taste?
but the pearls which swirl within the waves of
peppermint tea lakes
those waters of bated breath and happy drownings
forgoing our rowing, and remains
let these bodies burn by yells of yearn
until we are but ashes,
feathered on the crashes of hurricanes
our lungs the breeze,
giving wings to ghosts of flame
may our iris stars break the blue like thunder,
so angels might walk the seven wonders
allowing the rust of heaven's gates
paradise now exists upon my tongue

in words his arms have mused
in his moments my mention
shall not lose
heard in cellos of chartreuse,
a sweet song of sun
warmth that would grow a daisy's grin
among blades of pillows,
freckled fingers can be found combing in
sprouting strings which sway
to lullaby softer days
of threadless milky thistles,
thoughts waltzing on the wind.

- Molly Gentzsch
[@themusingsofmollymaven]

my mother taught me two things:
1. a woman possesses strength in her fist.

2. she knows when to unclench her jaw and release it.

(that is power)

- Mansi Jora
[@tiara.less]

in the name of love
they fooled her
into the arms of another

if only she had known
their desires would not care
for her bother

- *union*

- Janhavi Purkar
[@janwritesx]

she has that old-time charm.
that little bit of mystery that some
may have forgotten the importance of.
she wears long sleeves and loose skirts
so you have to dream about what is underneath.
wonder what her skin looks like,
and imagine how the dip in her hips
would feel between the clutch of your hands.
her hair is always all over her face.
it's regularly left in its natural state.
she's a mess.
but in her disorientation, is her balance.
in her crazy, is her sanity.
in those shadows, she finds light.
and in those memories, she finds life.
in all of those places of herself
that some may find unnerving
is where she finds, her freedom.
to be all things hypocritical,
to be all things broken,
and yet still to be
all things beautiful.

- Kaileigh Pfaff
[@kayf.j]

he puts his hands on me
and tells me it's love
so why does it hurt
in my bones, my soul
i'm watching the tears
run down my cheeks
as if i'm not even
in my body anymore
i'm just a discarded doll
lying bruised and used
in an unmade bed
what should have been heaven
is now hell and i can't escape
my legs are paralyzed
my mind numb, empty
trying to push his phantom hands
off my skin where they linger
like a tattoo that never really heals
he took everything from me
when he put his hands on me

- Helena Degn
[@helenadegnpoetry]

she is a
brutally soft
and gently powerful
kind of woman
the one
you meet
only once in a lifetime

- Lena Mora
[@iamlenamora]

i've finally learnt
the art of letting myself be
too much
too little
too loud
too quiet
too proud
too shy
i'm just letting myself be

- Shefali Dang
[@theshefalidang]

they always tell her she's too emotional
but it's the pouring instead of crying
the breaking instead of hurting
the shining instead of smiling
that make her the beautiful hurricane she is

she feels everything in extremes
you must experience all of her
to truly fathom the beauty of her heart

- Lindy van Hillo
[@lindy.v.h]

like the morning sun
(self) love will set us free;
the lifelong pursuit,
        a silent agreement.
forever is my promise to you,
i was born to fly
and not a day goes by
when i do not wait for the sun.
    the choice is mine (to hold on)
and sing a song for the desert skies
that remind me
of a different life.
like the morning sun after the long night,
i will rise.
i will set my soul free.
        (on self love)

- Cassandra Wood
  [@cm.writer]

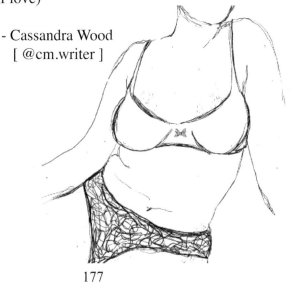

177

she emerged like a wisp of smoke,
curling through the air.

she left in the blink of an eye,
her essence forever lingering in the sky.

- Mansi Jora
[@tiara.less]

oh the chaos of being young, female and wild,
never dolled-up enough
and no rehearsal for this sham show
of depressing boxes.
i rather leap from them
into an uneven chorus;
the off-tune songs
sung along roads untravelled.
my ears hear the hymns,
the sweetest melodies,
beckoning me
to never dull myself under dark cloaks,
and instead welcome me into proud womanhood.

- Gigi Wickham
[@isorosawords]

my heart is exploding into a million love letters
that i wrote to myself
my words sing songs of self love
for today i've met myself
my search has come to an end
and now a new journey begins

- Shefali Dang
[@theshefalidang]

you look at my butt and breasts like they are objects
merely made for your recreation
i wish they would have told you in school
my body is not a station
for you to stop and then pass through

please, don't get too excited
i am not here for flirtation
because you are bored
or want me out of desperation
to add another name to your list

i am here to have fun with friends
not to offer you penetration
so look away and take your hands off my ass
because my body is not a vacation
it's a home.

- Lindy van Hillo
[@lindy.v.h]

the freedom of feminine intuition
as temperance dips
foot on land;
foot on water
pouring to a brimming chalice
with a dove-like freeness to feel.
i pity our counterparts
and their intact bottles,
until they are bursting anger,
while cries remain stifled
so they turn to hardened fists.
i've seen this before and can't help but fear
their touch.
i've learned not to trust male energy
quite young.
like a map, it takes time to locate the sweet kind.
so in the august daybreak i sit,
forever planning how to transcend this place.
how to find where field flowers
are nurtured for safekeeping
as the garden was by my father on sunday
mornings...
the most peaceful yard on the street.

- Gigi Wickham
[@isorosawords]

i was raised to be a flower
delicate and soft
but i was born to be
a queen
that is why my heart
is made of petals
and my will
is made of steel

- Shefali Dang
[@theshefalidang]

i am a warrior
fighting my battles
with stardust dripping from my veins;
i outshine the moon

- Marie Claire
[@s.m.claire]

accept yourself as you are,
now, in this moment,
and for who you may become
in the next.

- Cassandra Wood
[@cm.writer]

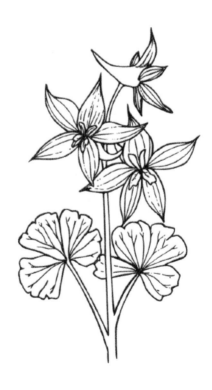

185

she is madness
melted in poetry
a war between
fire and peace
with a tremendous power
in her eyes made of galaxy

- Lena Mora
[@iamlenamora]

womanhood is
hearing the lectures of mountain strength,
and stone masonry
but knowing the cycling waves are just as forceful.
is that a glimpse of hysteria?
no, these rolling waters remain an enigma,
roaring as they cascade and change.
there must be more.
he as capable as her,
her as providing as he.
loving in peace, not fear.
her body is hers, not meat,
despite a different cannibalism
less punished;
always a wolf waiting,
its appetite weak and perverted.
hers, refined and patient if allowed to step into it;
the power of the moon and venus,
unwavering faith,
the strength of a lioness.

- Gigi Wickham
[@isorosawords]

society strives to make us
wary of other women,
tries its hardest to
portray us as selfish beings,
as wild things ravenous
for the blood of our own kind
but when i hit rock bottom,
i watched as women climbed
down from their thrones
to sit with me in the rubble.
then, when i was strong
enough to stand,
took me by the hand
and said,
"stay. this kingdom
is big enough for all of us."

- Sian RJ Wilmot
[@srwpoetry]

who i am is not your choice,
you do not get to define me
i will only be the woman
i want to, nothing more, nothing less.
   - as is, is enough

     - Cassandra Wood
      [@cm.writer]

189

she is sunny rain-boots landing in the puddle,
and she is the puddle too: easily shaken
serenely placed. she is ice cream in january,
a kiss of cool sugar amongst icy whips of wind.

she does not melt.
she is rhubarb pie with custard. you need
cool milk to wash her down. she pools
in stomachs like honey. good for your throat.
she'll soothe you when you're hurting.
and sometimes she is the hurt, the heartbreak,
the storm and the storm catcher. the crashing
rain and falling lights. pints of rocky road and
cases of plates thrown at empty walls. she is
broken into pieces on the floor.
but most of all, she is fairy light picnics
on the living room floor, with mandarin oranges
and buffalo chicken strips and ginger kombucha
that burns your throat going down. but it's a good
burn.

she is a good burn:

so loud, so angry and so very
warm.

- Arumann Dhillon
[@akdpoetry]

to the person who resents the storm inside their soul,

i wrote this for you. i was once close to getting out of this place because i couldn't bear the downpour in my heart, the thunder in my mind, the hurricane that was my existence. but i've always liked rainy days. something about the sky crashing to the earth in tiny droplets (nature's catharsis) is magical. i guess what i'm trying to say, is that no matter how much you are hurting, no matter how much you are trying to avoid the grief, the hurt, the anger, the exhaustion - you are not alone. the mightiest of beings feel in the most powerful of ways. if you cry lightning instead of tears, light up the sky.

- Cassandra Wood
[@cm.writer]

and if nothing else
please remember that you are *too much* for this
world in the best way possible,
do not conform to the expectations
they have set for you
just because they are not ready for all that you are
do not make yourself smaller for the sake of being
something they find digestible
you deserve more than that

- Elizabeth Todoroska
[@tipsyloveletters]

i will not be easily defined.
life is about change,
and through it i will take many forms,
proceeding without fear,
of who i may become.

- Cassandra Wood
[@cm.writer]

193

Acknowledgements

i want to thank each and every powerful woman who contributed to this publication. together, you are a strong and empowering voice for women around the world. your words will become a legacy for future generations of girls, whom i hope take your determined spirit and create change within worlds of their own.

Cassandra Mackenzie Wood

Canada

Aaisha
Hanif
Canada

Adelle
Woods
Australia

Alexandra
Michelle
United States

Arumann
Dhillon
Canada

E.J.
Sneed
United States

Elizabeth
Todoroska
Canada

Gigi
Wickham
Canada

Helena
Degn
Denmark

Janhavi
Purkar
Maylasia

Kaileigh
Pfaff
Canada

Lena
Mora
Kosovo / Sweden

Lindy
van Hillo
Netherlands

Mansi
Jora
India

Marie
Claire
Canada

Maryam
Asad
Pakistan

Molly
Gentzsch
United States

Shefali
Dang
Canada

Sian
Wilmot
United Kingdom

Chief Contributor and Editor

CM Writer, also known as Cassandra Mackenzie Wood, is a Canadian poet, novelist and storyteller born in 2002. Cassandra's collection includes two poetry anthologies, *The Roots of a Goddess* and *Wonder of the* Cosmos, several novels, and short prose. Along with these works, she is committed to sharing daily poetry on her Instagram platform @CM.Writer.

With the power of her words, Cassandra hopes to spread mental health awareness and advocate for social issues that impact the world today.

Printed in Great Britain
by Amazon

77418190R00113